AF427549

Faith: The Believer's Passport

✝ ✝ ✝

John Flanagan

Faith: The Believer's Passport
© 2022 John Flanagan

ISBN: 9798846553224

Scripture references are taken from The King James Bible

Printed in the USA

Table of Contents

1 "The End"

✝✝✝

The young seminary student was driving on the interstate, heading home from college. The radio was on. The program was suddenly interrupted by breaking news. From all sides, Israel was being attacked with no warning.

Outnumbered three to one, with a territorial area smaller than Hawaii, Israel would almost certainly be defeated. The student was shocked. If Israel no longer existed, then surely the prophesy would come to pass, maybe in minutes. His mind raced. What should he do? Quickly he pulled the car to the side of the road and waited patiently, excited. This was it! Surely, the rapture of the church would take place, and his parked car wouldn't hurt anyone when he disappeared in the blink of an eye.

It was 1967. The Six Day War had just started. Israel would go on to win that war convincingly and strengthen its strategic position. The student waited a long time before continuing the drive home. He lived out a normal life, founded a vibrant church, and was much used by God in his small community.

My question is, if you heard the same news while driving today as a Christian familiar with your Bible, would you park on the side of the road, and wait? What would you do?

The student acted in that moment because he believed God, His character, His Word, His promises to Israel, and His promises to His Church. He believed God. His belief resulted in action that day in 1967.

What about today? Jesus said, "Nevertheless when the Son of man comes, shall he find faith on the earth?"

Biblical faith is the subject of this work. What is it? How important is it? Do I have it? How do I get it?

2 To The Mature Christian

✝ ✝ ✝

"Then said they unto him, 'What shall we do, that we might work the works of God?' Jesus answered and said unto them, 'This is the work of God, that ye believe on him whom he hath sent.'" (John 6:28-29) Both the unsaved and saved are constantly pointed to that vital initial, and then ongoing, exercise of faith.

The Bible says, ". . . now is the day of salvation." (2 Cor 6:2) And it urges a person to put his faith in Christ as soon as possible.

My purpose in writing this booklet is to help Christians to a more vibrant spiritual life by means of *faith*. It is one of the most important words in the New Testament. Let me explain its importance in the following two short chapters.

3 What Is Faith/Believe?

✝ ✝ ✝

Why was the term *faith/believe* chosen? If *love* was the subject, this book would be about simply *love*. The English word *love* is like its corresponding Greek root word ΑΓΑΠ (AGAP)[1]. That one root word is used for both the verb and the noun. English speakers are not troubled by the grammatical uses of *love*, and have no difficulty switching from noun to verb, and back again.

For example:

John loves (v) Ann.

John has love (n) for Ann.

In English, the verb, *love*, and the noun, *love*, are the same word. In the same way, the Greek root word AGAP is understood to be the same word in its different forms, even

---

[1] Incomplete root words are in capital letters to distinguish them from complete words.

when used adjectivally or adverbially. It is the same basic concept and definition, and all grammatical forms are closely related.

But not so with the New Testament word for *faith/believe*. It is a linguistic anomaly in English that causes English speakers to think of *faith* and *believe* as two different words. In the New Testament, the original root word chosen by the Holy Spirit is ΠΙΣΤ (PIST). The verb form (πιστευω pisteuo) is usually translated *believe*, and the noun form (πιστις pistis) usually *faith*. But it is the same word in the original text, just different grammatical forms, very similar to *love* or AGAP.

Maybe you have heard someone say, "*Faith* is a noun." By this they mean that *faith* is a "**person, place, or thing**," as we learned in third grade. But Biblical *faith/believe* is both noun and verb. For ease of understanding in the rest of this booklet, *faith* and *believe* will sometimes be used interchangeably depending on the English sentence structure. But in each instance *faith/believe* would be more accurate because the New Testament word is both *faith* and *believe*.

When we hear, "*Faith* is a noun," what does that imply? Since faith is neither a place nor a person, it must mean that faith is a thing: an object, or quality. There are lots of objects in your life, a car, a house, a coin collection. How did you come to "have", or possess these things? Either you bought them, or stole them, or were given them. You see where this is leading. If faith is a thing, how do I get it? I can't buy it. Stealing is wrong. It must be given to me by God. But *faith* is not just a noun. It is not a thing. What is it? And just how important is it?

Faith: The Believer's Passport

4 Biblical Emphasis

$$\dagger \; \dagger \; \dagger$$

How important is *faith* in the New Testament? What are some of the most used words in the New Testament?

Theorem: Faith is the most significant word in the New Testament, other than the names of God.

What evidence can we find for the above statement? To start, we will look at the number of times the word occurs. We need to establish some ground rules. We will use the original words. (The textual basis is the 1894 Scrivener Textus Receptus.) For our purposes any serious Greek manuscript will do. Further, we will use root words. Greek words are very typically combined and varied in their word form. This is due to different word endings, prefixes, suffixes, and complex words.

We will not differentiate between the various parts of speech. The same root word is often used in noun, verbal, adjectival, and adverbial forms. Also, we will not consider the names of God, or unspecific building-block-type words such as articles, prepositions, and conjunctions (e.g. the, a, in, of, and, or, etc.)

So what root words are used the most in the New Testament original text?

The following is a list of the most used root words by occurrences:

1. Λεγω lego (say) ....3103 occ.
2. Ερχομαι erxomai (come or go).........................1425 occ.
3. Εχω exo (have) ....934 occ.
4. Διδωμι didomi (give)...692 occ.
5. Ποιεω poieo (do) ....640 occ.
6. Πιστις/πιστευω pistis/pisteuo (faith/believe).......609 occ.
7. Αγαπη/αγαπαω agape/agapao (love)...................320 occ.

Next, consider this list of the six most used words. (*Love* was added for comparison purposes and is out of order.) Four of these most used words (1,2,3,5) are simply descriptive. They are used to describe what happened in the New Testament. They tell the story. Ask yourself, as a Christian, which of these are most important for you and me to do today? Is the Bible emphasizing talking? Should I talk more? Come and go more? Have more? Give more? Do more? Believe more? Excluding *love* only two of these words are encouraged as specific exercises of the Christian life. They are *giving* and *believing*. The other four in our list are in most cases descriptive and intrinsic to telling the story. They are in the same category as conjunctions, articles, and prepositions. They are part of the background of language and serve as the setting for foreground communication.

Faith must be a very important word since it is one of the most used words in the New Testament.

Last, in verb form, it is often found in the imperative mood, being used as the key part of a command. Jesus said, "Let not your heart be troubled: ye believe in God, **believe** also in me." (John 14:1)

Believing may be the most important, and yet most misunderstood, Biblical concept in our present time. Therefore, it is vital that modern Christians have a better understanding.

5 Usage

✝ ✝ ✝

A word about usage: the fundamental concept of New Testament PIST is action. Even when the word is used in noun form the language is describing an action. If you are a baseball fan, you will be familiar with the noun, *hit*. Each professional player has a batting average. His average is the number of *hits* divided by the number of times he batted. A *hit* is when the player puts the ball fairly in play resulting in the player safely reaching any base. *Hit,* as a noun, most certainly describes an action, and is closely related to the verb, *hit*.

How can we tell that PIST is fundamentally an action? *Πιστις pistis* is in a class of nouns called **nouns of action**. "A noun of action is a noun the definition of which contains a verbal idea."[2] Romans 10:10 tells us that "with the heart man believeth (*πιστευω pisteuo*) unto salvation." There is an action that takes place in the heart of a person. With any transitive[3] action there is a subject initiating the action, and an object receiving the action. Babe Ruth hit the ball over the outfield fence. Babe Ruth is the subject, and the ball is the object. The Biblical paradigm of *faith* is this simple sentence from James 2:23. "And the scripture was fulfilled which saith, Abraham believed God, and it was imputed unto him for righteousness: and he was called the Friend of God." Abraham, the subject, acting in his heart, believed God, the object receiving the action.

This concept of action is also shown very precisely in the almost universal syntax used with the noun form, *pistis*. Usually, a noun of action is followed by a word in the genitive case. This genitive word which follows is technically **either** the subjective, or objective genitive. (There is a third option which we will not consider here, the plenary genitive.) In these cases, the noun is picturing a transitive action. The genitive word which follows shows **either** the subject or the object of the action. Bear with me.

---

[2] Brooks and Winbery, *Syntax of New Testament Greek* (Lanham, MD: University Press, 1979), 15.

[3] Transitive means that a verb takes a direct object, whether that object appears in the sentence, or is implied. *Faith/believe* typically has an object.

In English we have a similar form, which comes directly out of the Greek (and later Latin and French) to our language. The genitive case in Greek is often translated into English with the preposition *of*. In Ephesians 1:7, we find the English phrase "the forgiveness of sins." In the Greek, the phrase is αφεσιν των παραπτωματων, aphesis ton paraptomaton. The noun of action, forgiveness (αφεσις, from αφιημι which means to let go or forgive), is followed by the objective genitive, των παραπτωματων, or (the) sins. Who forgives what? Context says that it is God (subject) that forgives sins (object). In this case, the English translation flows naturally from the original Greek syntax and is well understood.

Another good example of this construction in English is the phrase "love of money." *Love* is also a noun of action and the prepositional phrase "of money" shows the object of the action, loving money. Biblical *love* always has a subject and object because Biblical love is an action. More on that later.

However, in English, some nouns, over time, have lost the idea of action. *Faith* is a good example. Because we no longer think of faith as describing an action we have lost the meaning in a verse like Galatians 2:20. When Paul says, "…And the life which I now live in the flesh I live by the faith of the Son of God," he uses *faith* (*pistis*) followed by the genitive case, Son of God. This is translated into KJV English as "faith of the Son of God." But our common twenty-first century understanding of the word *faith* is not

Faith: The Believer's Passport

that of an action. Therefore, some readers wrongly assume that Paul is talking about *faith* that belongs to or is possessed by Jesus. *Jesus owns faith. It is His.* This is incorrect. Paul is using a noun of action which is followed by a genitive case word, identifying **either** the subject **or** the object of the implied action. Back to the verse. Somebody believed someone. The subject **or** object of that believing, or faith, is Jesus. Obviously then, Jesus is the object, and Paul is the subject, who lives life by believing Jesus.

I do apologize for the technicality of the preceding paragraphs, but the main thing to get firmly in our heads and hearts is the Biblical principle that *faith* is an action. It takes place in the heart of a man or woman, actively and volitionally. It is not passive. It is not incidental or corollary to something else. It is not a byproduct. This action takes place in time and space. It is an event. It can be timestamped. It is as real as the moment the lovely bride says, "I do!" This Biblical principle of action is built into the language of the New Testament.

So how can we define this vital exercise in the Christian life? ***Faith* is an action which takes place in the human heart when a person places his or her trust in God and His Word.** It is personal, active, and definitive. It takes place in time and space. Man believes. It is active. It is not passive. Nor is it corollary.

Like AGAP or *love,* we conclude that the modern

English concepts of *love* and *faith* are upside down. To the Greek speaker of the first century AD the nouns, *love* and *faith*, are describing the actions of a person, whether seen or unseen. The verbal idea is preeminent.

But to the English speaker of the twenty-first century these nouns describe deeply felt emotion first and foremost. The verbs simply describe one's experience of these emotions.

The Holy Spirit chose first century Greek as the language of the New Testament. Modern English concepts of both *love* and *faith* are incorrect and misleading when applied to Biblical truth.

6 Not Righteousness

✝✝✝

But how can a sinner believe God? The Bible says that Abraham believed God, and it (faith/belief) was counted to him for righteousness. All human beings born after Adam are sinners by nature, from birth. We all have sinned. Each one of us has broken God's law of righteousness. (I wish to point out that this does not mean that every single human action is sinful. A murderer typically does not murder everyone he meets. The fact that we sin does not mean that we are incapable of any act of righteousness.)

Getting back to Abraham, he believed, but his believing was **not** an act of righteousness. God chose to count it for righteousness. Again, it was **NOT** righteousness. God made a way, a path, for man to admit his sin and be forgiven. The cause or trigger for releasing God's priceless provision in one's life is faith.

My house has many, many electrical devices. For this

reason, there is a distribution system in place. This system is connected to a local distribution network of power lines and transformers. These lines are connected to a local substation. The substation is connected to large transmission lines which then are connected to a power generation plant that is over a hundred miles away. When the sun goes down, the house gets dark. To remedy this, I simply walk to the wall and flip a switch which then lights the room. A huge amount of work and cost has gone into the power plant, the transmission lines, the substation, the power lines, and my residential electrical wiring. A huge effort is ongoing to maintain this vast power system. But when the sun goes down, I must flip the switch to have light. It is useless for me to sit in my chair and hope that the power company will make the room light up. Action is required. The switch is inexpensive. It is nothing in the scheme of things. A soft drink at McDonalds costs more than a switch. But if I do not **act** and flip the switch, I will continue to sit in the dark.

Faith is like my living room light switch. It is nothing. It is not righteousness. It is not the priceless sacrifice. It is not worthy of any praise. It did not take my punishment. It is not the source of resurrection power. It cannot keep me safe in times of hardship and temptation. But unless I actively believe today, none of those things will be a part of my experience of God today. I must, in my heart, **live** by **believing** God today! I must flip the switch . . . Gal 2:20 says

I live by *faith* in Jesus. Romans 1:17 says, The just shall live by *faith*. The unsaved are saved by *faith*, and the saved are to live continuously by *faith*.

God has provided the work, the sacrifice, the righteousness, and the means for mankind to access His Great Provision. The means is our *faith/believe* in Him. He made a way for us to receive His Great Provision, and we need every bit of what He has provided. John 1:12 says, "But as many as received Him, to them gave He power to become the sons of God, even to them that *believe* on His name." God made a way for us to receive Him. How? *Faith/believe*.

***Faith* is not righteousness.** This truth must be emphasized. In fact, it cannot be emphasized too much. When a man or woman believes the Lord and what God's Word says, that action which takes place in one's heart is **NOT** a work of righteousness. Abraham believed God and it was counted to him for righteousness. *Faith/believe* is not a work. Paul does not confuse *faith* with works. Neither does James. *Faith* is, to use the theological term, non-meritorious. It has no intrinsic moral value. *Faith* is not a work. *Faith* and works are mutually exclusive.

"What!" you say. "But if one believes, he will live a righteous life," you say. I agree with you to a point. Righteousness should result from *faith/believe* in God and His Son. When we believe we are born again and receive a new nature. We become new creations in Christ. This new nature is righteous and will always do what is right. (Unfortunately, while we live on this earth the old sinful nature is also active within us.) But works are the **results** of *faith* in God, His Son, and His Word. *Faith* is not righteousness.

In fact, *faith/believing* in Jesus is, in a profound way, just the opposite of a work of righteousness. We come to God precisely because we have learned that we are not righteous. We have broken God's Law. We are sinners. We are incapable of keeping God's standard of righteousness. Therefore, we come to Christ. As Peter said, Where else can we go? Only One paid the price. Only One offers forgiveness. Only One can prevail upon the Father to receive us. Only One is worthy. We are not. Only One pleases the Father. We do not. We put our trust in that One! *Believing* this One means we no longer trust in ourselves. God made a way for us to come that is not a work. *Believe*! He is calling us to believe, now!

7 A Word About Our Culture

✝ ✝ ✝

It is very difficult for one to escape the assumptions, presuppositions, and underlying philosophies of one's present culture. We all bring to each decision, thought, and conversation a common viewpoint. It is notoriously hard to escape this often uncritical, even subconscious, lens through which we see our experience and the experiences of others.

There is one aspect of our current culture which bears very heavily on the modern Christian's view of *faith/believe*. This is the overwhelming **emotionalization** of all experience and thought in the twenty-first century. Notice how often, even in professional correspondence, a person (like an architect,) expressing a professional opinion about a current decision, says something like, "I **feel** strongly that the budget for your new front door is twenty percent too low." Words mean something. Yes, he is trying to diplomatically tell the customer that he has underestimated the cost of a new entry door system. He is trying to soften the blow, but is the budget an emotional decision, an emotional discussion? He should raise the budget because . . . his architect has a strong feeling? My guess is that this imaginary interchange is not that shocking to my reader. It sounds like a normal way of talking precisely because we are so greatly influenced by our culture. For comparison, please imagine the NASA engineers discussing the trajectory of the first manned Mercury rocket in the early sixties. The leader of the trajectory group would not say, "I **feel** strongly that the rocket will be too heavy and might undershoot the target area." Professional discussions in the Sixties were, well . . . professional, empirical, and typically did not include emotional descriptions.

As another example, this author read a recent article in the local newspaper. High school bullying was the subject. A school counselor was quoted as saying, "It is not what you say that is important, but rather how what you say makes the other person feel that is important." In other words, verbal content is secondary to the primary goal of human communication which is emotion. Again, it is very difficult to completely escape the constraints of our culture. To some extent all of us are influenced and even controlled by the culture in which we live. The counselor's statement would be regarded with complete shock by great thinkers of the past. Our present age is the age of visual and emotional understanding. We have moved away from a verbal and rational understanding of our world. The previous age was one of words and logic. Ours is one of pictures, video, and emotion. In previous times, people **read** the news. Today we **watch** the news. "The medium is the message," (Marshall McLuhan.) The newspaper conveyed verbal truth. Just read a newspaper from a hundred years ago. Written for the everyday reader you will find complex sentences centered on the facts. Typical print headlines today are often speculative what-if imaginings with the goal—an emotional reaction. Much of what passes for television news is video with music and comments. Maybe this? Could it be? What if? Headlines go like this: Experts say that ______ may ______. Example: A group of scientists concur that ocean levels could raise three feet by 2050. First, the group quoted is speculating on what might happen. This is not actually news. Second, there is another group of scientists that think the first group is all wet. Third, if you live in South Florida, and lots of people do, they will read the article and put money in the pockets of the writers and scientists. Fourth, the goal is an emotional reaction on the part of the reader, or watcher. If the report makes it to the evening news, the video will likely be accompanied by pictures of large waves wiping out property somewhere for some reason unrelated to general global sea level rise. The point is the pictures, video, and sound effects are right out of Hollywood, and carefully combined for their emotional effect. And this is the culture in which we live and breathe every day. We all, to some degree, think more emotionally than previous generations, and therefore less rationally.

So, what does this have to do with living the Christian life? Just this: We see Biblical concepts through the lens of our culture. A Greek speaker in 100 A.D. reads the words: The just shall live by faith. He understands faith (pistis) to be an action in one's heart with a subject, oneself, and an object, God. This fits perfectly with another statement in the Bible that Abraham believed (pisteuo) God. (Same root word.) This same action takes place in Abraham's heart at a moment in time when he, the subject, places his faith and trust in God, the object of his believing, or faith. *Faith* as a noun describes an action. The event is deliberate, active, and decisive. It is objectively real within a specific timeframe.

In contrast, an English speaker in the twenty-first century reads these same verses. He has several disadvantages. He is reading English, he does not know Greek, and he lives in a very different culture. What he understands is very different from the first-century reader above. "The just shall live by *faith.*" *Faith*, to him, is a noun like love. It is an emotion, a feeling, a mood. Emotions come and go in his experience. God must give him faith. He cannot work it up. He either has it or he doesn't. God must bring him to the moment when he suddenly realizes that he has come to trust in God. The event is passive, overwhelming, and emotionally satisfying.

He may have had a previous experience where he was overcome by intense emotion like joy—a feeling of closeness toward God. As Christians we all covet those wonderful times. And we cannot manufacture them whenever we want. But that closeness, with its intense emotional component, is **not** faith/believe. Why would God in His word constantly encourage both the unsaved and the saved to believe **now** if faith is an emotional experience which only God can produce at any given time? "And this is the will of him that sent me, that every one which seeth the Son, and *believeth* on him, may have everlasting life: and I will raise him up at the last day." (John 6:40)

It is helpful to compare this emotional view of faith with another similar New Testament word, *love. Love* (agape) is also a noun of action with a subject and an object. But modern culture thinks of love almost exclusively as an emotion. In the twenty-first century love happens. The poor unsuspecting young man is smitten by Cupid's arrow. He is overwhelmed. He no longer thinks rationally. In fact, the irrationality of love is a great part of the enjoyment.

He is swept away. The event is passive, overwhelming, and irresistible. But it is obvious that this model creates problems. What if the young man has fallen for a married woman? What if the woman does not love her husband? Oh, she used to. But now the thrill is gone. As we see throughout our culture, this Hollywood picture of love is unsustainable. It cannot last and we know it. We experience it every day. An acquaintance is turning forty and has worked his way through five marriages and who knows how many girlfriends. The "emotion" of love, comes and goes—so do the relationships. But Christians know better don't they? They have God's Word.

Unfortunately, the statistics are not much different for Christians. Why? Because we have a wrong concept of love. *love* is supposed to be an action we do. We chose to love. Work at it! I don't mean for a moment that marital love should be devoid of emotion, but Biblical love, for spouse, children, friends, fellow believers, and the unsaved, is active, decisive, and deliberate. If love is an emotion, then I wait and see. If love is an action for me to take, I must engage in this wonderful activity. I must love, **now**.

So, we see that the emotionalization of Biblical concepts tends to result in a passive Christian lifestyle. We are waiting for our favorite TV program with its associated thrill. Passive. And we are waiting for God to move us to greater faith and love. Passive! But the Bible is telling **us** to believe now, to love now. Go ahead. O taste and see that the Lord is good: blessed is the man that trusts Him. Don't be the slothful man that puts his hand to the dish of food but will not raise his hand and put the food in his mouth. And the implication is that when we taste we will experience His goodness and finish the meal.

As we actively trust and believe Him, only then will we have all that the Good Shepherd has planned for us. Only then will we live in the Promised Land of victory, and eat the fruit of the land, and put off the deeds of the flesh. Walls will fall, and so will giants. We live by faith. *Believe*. Now! Today! Abraham believed God. Will you? David put his trust in the Lord (Ps. 31:1). Will you?

8 Common Misconceptions:

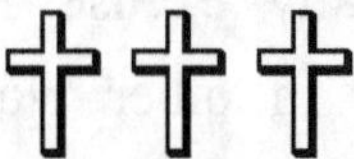

    This chapter addresses some common misconceptions about faith. Each bold and italicized heading below is a misstatement about Biblical faith. Italicized words are further explanations of the misconception. Then follows a section for the reader's consideration. I can pretty much guarantee that one or more of these misconceptions has some influence on the reader, and that exposing them may create consternation and possibly even anger. My hope is that prayerful thought will result in a better understanding in the long term and a closer walk with God. I apologize in advance if my writing upsets some readers.

Faith is mental assent. *Robert N. Wilkin has written that*

faith occurs when overwhelming evidence is presented to the mind. According to him the moment that this evidence is processed and accepted is the moment that faith occurs. "...Faith is not a decision. It is the conviction that something is true." (Confident in Christ, P. 6) In his view lack of faith is simply lack of sufficient evidence.

Consider: Biblically, no one will, finally, at the judgement day have any excuse for not believing and therefore being saved. In other words, God has already presented sufficient evidence. As Jesus said, "It is finished." There are four witnesses: creation, human nature, God's Word, and Jesus Himself, the man who stands in time, space, and history. To place Biblical faith in God on the same level as belief in the existence of atoms is missing the essence of Biblical faith and therefore missing salvation, forgiveness, eternal life, and fellowship with God.

The reader may have heard of the great tightrope walker, Charles Blondin. In 1859, he stretched a special, made-for-the-occasion, 1100' rope across the Niagara Falls gorge. A huge crowd gathered for the occasion. Standing at one end of the rope he asked if anyone thought he could carry a man across the falls on his back. Silence ... He then surprised everyone by running full speed out over the falls on the rope. Later, he did take his manager on his back across the falls. On other days he did all kinds of stunts. He walked on stilts. He took a stove and cooked an omelet. He crossed blindfolded. He did a handstand. He pushed a wheelbarrow full of rocks. After this last trick he then asked the crowd if they believed that he could push a man across the falls in the same wheelbarrow. They yelled, "Yes!" Charles then asked for a volunteer! No one spoke. Then a man stepped forward! That man got the ride of his life. Blondin successfully took the man across the Falls!

In the same way we put our trust in the God-That-Is-Able. We have skin in the game. Every believer is putting his eternal fate in the hands of Jesus. Biblical *faith/believe* is personal, decisive, and focused on God, His Son, and His Word. It can never be just an automatic, passive, mental reaction to overwhelming evidence.

According to this misconception, doubt is justified until God proves himself. It is up to God to persuade me. If I'm not convinced, God hasn't done His job. It's up to Him to convince me.

But Jesus said, For God so loved the world, that he gave his only begotten Son, that whosoever believeth in him should not perish, but have everlasting life. We are called upon to believe in Jesus. We are to put our faith in Him. Today is the day of salvation. There is evidence, but it is not the evidence itself that we trust. We believe Him. Abraham believed God . . .

Faith is obedience. *I believe that this misconception grows out of the general confusion about what faith actually is. It is also appealing to those parts of Christendom that are more comfortable with a list of dos and don'ts than fellowship with the Almighty. A well-known Christian leader said, "Just do right."*

Consider: Like Adam after the fall, the legalist looks for a way to quickly cover his shame. Yes, the legalist sinned yesterday, but today he did 1,2,3; and didn't do 4,5,6. Of course the problem is that the list is phony. The legalist's righteousness is just the repackaged false righteousness of the Pharisees.

Jesus is the true standard. The only way a man can achieve that standard is Jesus Himself living through him by faith. Faith cannot be obedience. Obedience is keeping God's law, living up to His standard, which was only fulfilled by Jesus. Obedience is equivalent to works, and faith and works are mutually exclusive.

Faith is a gift. *This misconception has its roots in the*

English translation of Ephesians 2:8. "For by grace are ye saved through faith; and that not of yourselves: it is the gift of God . . ." What is the gift of God? **It.** *What is* **it** *referring to?* **It** *refers to* **that.** *What is* **that** *referring to? According to English rules of grammar, the pronoun* **that** *refers to the nearest antecedent, which would be "faith."*

Consider: This is one of the times where one can see why God decided that the New Testament would be written in Greek and not English. Greek pronouns do not follow the same rules. Greek can clearly do something that English cannot. English is a word-order language. Greek uses word order in most cases for emphasis only. Greek word endings tell the respective parts of speech and how each word relates to the other. **That** in the verse is neuter gender. Therefore, **that** must refer to a neuter antecedent. But the words **grace** and **faith** are feminine gender! Therefore, **that** cannot refer to either **grace** or **faith**. Instead, the neuter pronoun, **that,** refers to the entire phrase built around the verb **saved**. Therefore, the gift is the entire process of salvation! By God's grace, not our works of righteousness; through *faith/believe*, the cause, switch, not the source; we are saved. "Whosoever shall call upon the name of the Lord shall be saved." We call with our mouth in prayer as we *faith/believe* in our hearts: unto righteousness, His righteousness; and salvation, eternal life with Him.

Faith is a substance. This misconception is based on Hebrews 11:1. Many have taken this verse to be a definition of faith. Faith is therefore a substance. This misconception views faith as something like courage. We say that one has great courage. By this we mean that one typically acts with little regard for personal safety when fulfilling his duties to a higher authority or ideal. This language pictures courage as something, a substance or quality, which one simply possesses. The problem with this picture, and it may or may not be accurate regarding courage, is that there is no means of getting courage. One just has it, or not. Even on the subject of courage, this view seems to minimize the many desperate decisions which brave men and women make all the time—as if choosing to attack an enemy that has the high ground was in fact somewhat easy, I mean the choosing not the attacking, given that God just happened to make me courageous. But what if I am afraid? Did God just choose to make me a coward? Is there no way for me to get courage? The Cowardly Lion at least had hope that the Wizard of Oz might be able to grant him courage. But where can I go for courage? You either have it or you don't.

Faith is like that for many. They think of faith as a

substance or quality which is either a part of their personality, or not.

Consider: *Faith* is the substance of things hoped for… The Greek word is ὑποστασις, hupostasis, which means something that supports and stands under something else. The picture is of a column or foundation, *faith/believe*, which undergirds the things that we Christians hope for. *Faith* supports things that are hoped for. **2Pe 1:4** "Whereby are given unto us exceeding great and precious promises: that by these ye might be partakers of the divine nature, having escaped the corruption that is in the world through lust." God gave promises, like where we will spend eternity. Because we actively *faith/believe* Him and His promises, we also have sure hope that we will be with Him in heaven for eternity. Our hopes are supported by *faith/believe* in Him and His promises. The first part of the verse is describing a result of faith, which is hope.

Faith is . . . the evidence of things not seen. The Greek word for evidence is ελεγχος, elegxos, pronounced ele<u>n</u>kos. The word refers to the evidence that convicts in court. In our common parlance, it could be referred to as the *smoking gun.* So, *faith/believe* not only supports our hopes, but it also provides proof of things that are not seen. The fact that *faith/believe*rs are willing to go all over the world proclaiming Christ and even dying for *faith/believe* in Him is evidence that God exists, even though we cannot see Him.

Faith: The Believer's Passport

By extension our *faith/believe* is also evidence for the explanations of reality found in God's Word. Scientists may have theories about creation, but no one was there to observe it.

So let us revisit the verse, Hebrews 11:1. "Now faith is the substance of things hoped for, the evidence of things not seen." We now see *faith/believe* supporting our hopes, and validating the unseen reality in which we live, especially the Biblical account of Things. So, the verse seems more an explanation of what *faith/believe* does rather than a definition of what it is. *Faith/believe* results in hope and certainty. But *faith/believe* is not equivalent to hope and certainty. This makes sense considering the entire chapter, which lists forty results of faith. See appendix.

So, *faith/believe* is not a trait or personal attribute that one either has or has not. If it were, then where would one go to get it? The obvious answer would be God.

This misconception again points in the direction of action by God. God gives faith, period. That's it. If I don't have it, it is because God didn't give it to me. I need faith, but it is God's move.

But the Biblical emphasis is on the finished work of God the Father and the Son, and it is up to *man* to *faith/believe* in God, who has already provided all the necessary and sufficient requirements for us to *faith/believe*. Biblically, it is not God's move; it is ours! We must and should actively *faith/believe* in the One who has already proved Himself: His existence, His love, and His great sacrifice for us.

Faith is passive. This misconception grows out some of the combined misconceptions above. If you think faith is a result of God's irresistible persuasion, if you think faith is an emotion, if you think faith is a personal attribute, if you think faith is an unseen substance; then you see faith as something that happens to you. The experience is passive.

Consider: But the Bible emphasizes our need to believe God. It is the overwhelming emphasis of the New Testament. Again, with the heart **man** believes. **Now** is the day of salvation. We are saved by faith, and we live by faith. It is our move. Christ has been lifted up. God has drawn all men unto Himself. It is finished. It's man's move. *Faith/believe* is not passive. It is active! Abraham believed God. The verse does not say that God caused Abraham to believe Him. Remember: *Faith/believe* is not a work of righteousness. It is nothing. We are putting our *faith/believe* in God. It is the one and only thing that we can do.

Faith: The Believer's Passport

Faith is a corollary. *This misconception is actually an article of one school of Theology. Within this group a man is unable to believe God until God causes that specific man to be born again. The man is regenerated by fiat of God, and then, as a result, the man, because of his new nature, automatically has saving faith and prays to receive Christ. This theological view makes faith/believe an automatic and corollary result of being regenerated by the fiat of God. Through no decision, thought, or conscious action the man is suddenly a new creature, and then he prays and receives Christ by faith.*

Consider: But then why does the New Testament emphasize the necessity of man *faith/believing*? To this writer the Biblical concept of *faith/believe* is difficult to reconcile with this school of theology. The two seem incompatible. Either man actively *faith/believe*s, or there is no need for the lessons on, and exhortations to *faith/believe*.

✝ ✝ ✝

Faith is a leap. *This misconception is right out of our culture. Some say that there are facts, and then there are beliefs. Facts are verifiable. Accepting facts, data, and statistics that are documented is rational. On the other hand, beliefs are unverifiable and are by definition irrational. They* *are opinions and preferences with no basis in the real, material world. These statements are widely accepted in our materialistic, scientific world.*

Consider: But all humans live their lives based on presuppositions that cannot be verified. In the area of Symbolic Logic, Godel's Theorems of Incompleteness prove that a complete system of logic must have at least two assumptions which cannot be proved to be true within the system. Even the cold rationalist lives a full personal life with intangibles like love of family, or country. There could be much discussion on this topic but the point, as regards *faith/believe* is that *faith is often viewed as irrational. One living by faith must LEAP from the world of facts into a medieval world of unverifiable ghosts, spirits, gods, and demons. Thus comes the phrase, "Leap of Faith."*

This is not Biblical *faith/believe*. God has provided evidence: the creation, man, the Bible, and Jesus Himself. Isn't it interesting that the present high-tech, materialistic, scientific world in which we live is still fascinated with the unseen world? Imagination is king in Hollywood, and their imaginary worlds sell! But Biblical *faith/believe* is not a leap. It is firmly grounded on God, His works, and His Word. Our Christian faith is not irrational, but completely reasonable.

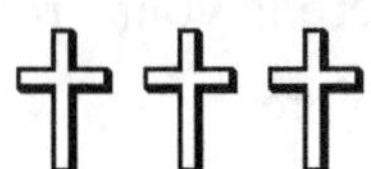

Faith: The Believer's Passport

*There are two kinds of faith. Picture three neighbors: Adam, Bob, and Cal. Adam shared the gospel with Bob, and Bob accepted Christ. He put his trust in Jesus, and prayed for Him to forgive him and grant him eternal life. Adam tells Cal that Bob has met the requirements of Romans 10 and is saved, born again. Sometime later Cal comes to Adam and tells him that Bob does not seem to be a Christian. Why? Because he does not attend church three times a week, and he has a bad habit or two, and he uses bad language sometimes. He just does not measure up to the current stereotypical Christian image. Bob goes on like this for a few years. Cal finally says that Bob is definitely not a Christian. But Adam says that Bob put his faith in Jesus. He prayed. He said he believed God. To this, Cal says that there are two kinds of faith. Yes, Bob put faith in Jesus, but it was (obviously) not **saving** faith. In other words, there are two kinds of faith: regular or common faith, and **saving** faith.*

Consider: It is like saying there are two kinds of gasoline: regular gasoline, and **combustible** gasoline. Imagine if you went down to the gas station and put in regular gasoline, but the car would not start. You complain to the people working there that the gasoline is no good. They ask if you put in regular. You say, "Yes."

They say, "Well there is your problem. You should have put in **combustible** gasoline."

You say, "But I thought all gasoline was combustible!"

"Oh no," they say. "There are two kinds of gasoline!"

Obviously a gas station trying this kind of subterfuge would not last long. The owner would be fined or in jail in short order. But some are trying to say that there is faith in God that does not actually result in salvation. Why is believing God in one's heart not sufficient for salvation? Some say, "Because your heart must be regenerated first."

There has been nothing more personally heartbreaking in my life than to hear a teenage young man, raised in a pastor's home, say, "I want to believe in God, and I want to be saved, but God has not yet given me **saving** faith." The Bible says, "Now is the day of salvation." *Believe*! But for this young man a great misconception is keeping him from simply praying and receiving Christ by *faith/believe* **now**! *For him, it is God's move.* But Biblically, the young man must himself in his heart believe in the God who has done **all** already. I pray this misconception will be corrected for my friend before it is too late.

9 Calvinism's Changed Emphasis

This author's study of *faith* has led him to a rather controversial position. If *faith/believe* is one of the most important activities of the Christian Life, if it is an action which takes place in the heart of man, if it is a non-meritorious and transitive action with an individual man as subject and God as object, if all this is true; then the current widespread teachings of Calvinism or Reformed Theology seem to have erred in a fundamental way. To the modern church under the sway of this school of Theology, faith is a passive experience, a corollary result of God's sovereign work in each individual Christian. *Faith* is something that happens to some and not to others and is completely out of any human's control.

But the Biblical portrayal of and exhortation to *believe* is not at all passive. God, the prophets, Jesus, the apostles, and New Testament writers ask, encourage, and command *man* to *believe* God. They encourage **all** men to *believe*. They ask individuals to *believe* now. Romans 10:8, "But what saith it (Deuteronomy 30)? The word is nigh thee, even in thy mouth, and in thy heart: that is, **the word of faith**, which we preach; . . ." The word of faith that Paul preaches isn't the passive, wait-for-it modern misconception. New Testament *faith* affirms that *faith* is "nigh thee." God made a way for you to be saved now. You do not have to look for it in the depths of the sea. You do not have to search the sky for it. It's in your mouth and your heart! Your mouth is able to pray. Your heart is able to believe. Act in your heart! *Believe*! Work your mouth! Confess Jesus! Pray! Receive Him!

So, compare for yourself, reader, Biblical *faith* with the passive, byproduct faith you may have been taught. *Believe* and pray, and you will be saved. Christian, live by *faith*. Trust Him actively today, and you will live by faith with resurrection power in the land of victory. Heb 4:9, "There remaineth therefore a *rest* to the people of God." Follow Him. *Believe*! Live by faith!

The Bible exhorts "believers" to sow God's Word and become "fishers of men." But some wish to talk to men occasionally "as God gives opportunity" about Biblical principles, but any urgency to pull the net and with it the man out of the waters of death into the boat of eternal life is missing, because they see themselves as having very little to do with regeneration, a man being born again.

Have you ever discovered termite damage? Have you looked at a very visible painted piece of wood for years assuming it to be sound because it appeared so, only to find one day that a large chunk of "sound" wood has come off? For years the termites have taken infinitesimal bites out of that wood, working beneath the surface in darkness, oh so slowly, consuming your house until all that is left is a very thin layer of wood and two or three coats of paint! Years earlier, if you had known where to look, you could have gone to the first small area of damage and dealt with it. But the surface looked fine. It was below the surface that the problem occurred.

The whole question of which comes first, faith in Christ or new birth, seems on the surface to be only a doctrinal technicality. But when they are switched, the reversed emphasis begins to eat away at Biblical *faith*, a primary catalyst in both salvation *and* sanctification.

Faith: The Believer's Passport

10 Imperfect Faith

✝ ✝ ✝

God made a way for man to receive salvation. That way is *faith/believe*. It is the cause of, or trigger for releasing God's tremendous, priceless provision to redeem man. I didn't make it that way; God did. *Faith/believe* is like the switch mentioned earlier. It is nothing. The great emphasis is God's provision, His Son, Jesus. *Faith/believe* is focused on the object, the Savior. But *faith/believe* itself is not the focus. Even minute faith is enough. *Faith* as a grain of mustard seed is accepted. It will result in the removal of mountains. Little faith was enough for Peter to walk on water. Do you think that you must have perfect, amazing faith with not a shadow of doubt in order for God to do great things in your life? The very question puts the emphasis on *faith* itself. That cannot be! The proper focus is Jesus. He will save you! He will help you! He paid the price for you! He loves you! Always, the focus is Him, not me, not you, and certainly not the quality of our faith. *Faith* is nothing, like the switch. But if the switch is off, there is no light, no power. *Believe* in Him!

David prayed in the Psalms many times, "In thee O Lord do I put my trust." We know this because he wrote it down. His prayer is a written statement. As the saying goes, "Put it in writing!" Did he write it for us? Maybe so. But his prayer is a contract with God. David is declaring his present, active *faith/believe* in God.

Faith is hard to see. One *believes* in one's heart. Then the enemy comes along and says, "You really aren't trusting God completely, perfectly, sufficiently." He roars! But in answer, David simply writes down this statement of fact. I trust you, God. That's it. The switch is on. God's power is released. Satan is defeated. Something as small and insignificant as a mustard seed took care of that old serpent. *Believe* in God. Do it like David. "Put it in writing!" Do it like Abraham, Peter, Paul, and all the rest of the heroes of Hebrews 11.

11 Is Faith/Believe Hard?

This author has heard many statements about faith over the years. Some fall into this category. One says, "*Faith* is hard!" Another, "I reject Easy Believism!"

By way of explanation, the following is a typical statement about Easy Believism:

> *Easy believism is a somewhat derogatory term used by opponents of the view that one needs only to believe in Jesus in order to be saved. From this they conclude that those who hold to sola fide ("faith alone") teach that no corresponding need exists for a committed life of Christian discipleship as proof of salvation; however, that is not what sola fide means. True faith in Christ will always lead to a changed life. Another common usage of the term easy believism is in regards to those who believe*

> *they're saved because they prayed a prayer—with no real conviction of sin and no real <u>faith</u> in Christ. Praying a prayer is easy—thus the term easy believism—but there is more to salvation than mouthing words.*
> *https://www.gotquestions.org/easy-believism.html*

So, the term should really be Easy Prayism, rather than Easy Believism!

If I understand the writer, those against Easy Believism are concerned that a person can only be saved by praying, believing, and then proving their salvation by living a holy life. How holy is anyone's guess. One must exhibit "a changed life." I am all for holy living, and a "changed life," assuming that the person in question was previously a serial killer, drug addict, or prostitute. If he simply exaggerated the truth and drank alcohol sometimes in his law practice, I would assume that not much **visible** change would be required (for proof of salvation.) And who is inspecting this change? If the person in question was the deacon of a large denominational church before he was saved, I would further assume that there would not be much change at all in the externals of his life.

But Biblically, the means of salvation is confession (or agreement, prayer) with the mouth, and *faith/believing* in the heart, per Romans 10. "Praying a prayer" or "mouthing words" without believing in one's heart cannot save a person, but "praying a prayer," **and** *faith/believing* in one's heart will save every single time! As Paul says, "This is the word [or message] of faith which we preach."

Salvation and the means of salvation is a vital subject, but what we are interested in is *faith/believe*. Is faith really hard? Some Calvinists think faith is actually impossible until God by fiat regenerates a person, and then gives them faith to be saved. Before they are born again, they cannot pray and believe and be saved. Some from this school prevaricate with terms such as common faith versus saving faith. See two kinds of faith above. To them faith, saving faith, isn't just hard. It is impossible. It is done by God through regeneration with absolutely no human action or participation. (Think about that for a minute or two.)

But there are those who seriously view faith for a sanctified Christian as "hard." Is *faith/believing* hard? The Biblical view seems to me to be that *faith/believe* for both the saved and the unsaved is designed by God for the powerless, the weak, and the inadequate. If you read through the list of forty things in Hebrews 11 that result from *faith/believe*, not a one of them is **easy**. Is it easy to face the fiery furnace, stop the mouth of lions, to bear a child after menopause, to stop the rain for three-and-one-half years? Is it easy to walk on water? These are all beyond the power of a man or woman. Yet these heroes accomplished them "by faith."

Faith: The Believer's Passport

Is it hard to move three thousand pounds of steel, aluminum, and plastic with one foot? If your foot is resting on the accelerator of a car, it isn't. Push down and you can even make the car move faster than a racehorse. Pushing the car eighty miles per hour isn't hard at all with one's foot on the accelerator!

Yes, it is hard to face the fiery furnace, but it is not hard to *faith/believe* God. The true *faith/believer* is not trusting in his courage or ability to do amazing things. He is trusting God, His Word, His Son, His Holy Spirit, and His resurrection power to accomplish these impossible tasks. The focus is on Him! He will accomplish the task. He is **all** power. It is easier to rely on His power than relying on your car. *Faith/believe* is **easy**. He made it that way so that even a weak, timid person like me can do it. Trust Him! Follow Him!

12 Little Faith, Great Faith

✝ ✝ ✝

There are descriptions of faith in the Bible that tend to make us think of faith in a quantitative way. Jesus tells Peter, after pulling him from the water, "O thou of **little faith**, wherefore didst thou doubt?" Does this mean that Peter's faith is small? Is Jesus rebuking Peter? Another time the disciples wake Jesus as He sleeps in the boat during a great storm. "Lord, save us: we perish," they say. Jesus responds, "Why are ye fearful, O ye of **little faith**?" Then He arose, and rebuked the winds and the sea; and there was a great calm. (Matthew 8:25-6)

Twice Jesus praises those who believe. Matthew 8:10, "When Jesus heard it [the centurion who believed,] he marveled, and said to them that followed, 'Verily I say unto you, I have not found so **great faith**, no, not in Israel.'" And also: Matthew 15:28, "Then Jesus answered and said unto her, 'O [Syrophoenician] woman, **great is thy faith**: be it unto thee even as thou wilt.' And her daughter was made whole from that very hour." Jesus is amazed and praises these two, but why? In Matthew 8:10 we get a clue. He says, ". . . no, not in Israel." Compare the disciples' little faith to the great faith of the centurion and Syrophoenician woman. First, consider the disciples. They are Jews native to Israel. They have been taught the Old Testament since they were children. One would expect them to have a much better understanding of theology, and therefore of God, since theology is the study of God. I don't mean that they were highly educated men, though some of them probably were. But they were familiar with the Bible of the time and probably had been required to read the entire Old Testament. They were almost certainly regular attenders at the local synagogue. Then consider the centurion and Syrophoenician woman. They were not Jewish. They had not grown up reading the Old Testament. They were gentiles. Their upbringings would have been filled with Greek and Roman culture, mythology, and philosophy. They had not known the God of Israel their whole lives.

Given the great advantages the disciples had, one would expect them to *faith/believe* Jesus daily. They should have been expecting great, amazing, awesome happenings with Jesus all the time! They lived with Him. They were in His presence 24/7, or nearly so. The confidence that Jesus had with His Father should have resulted in the disciples' confidence in Jesus. They should have had **great** *faith/believe*! But instead, they had just a **little** *faith/believe*. But consider, what was the result of "little faith?" Peter walked on water! The disciples saw winds gusting to forty miles per hour, and ten-foot waves disappear in an instant! (Rough estimates only.) Have you walked on water? Have you seen a storm turn calm in an instant? These are the results of even "little faith." Oh, that we might see more of even little faith.

Matt. 17:20, "And Jesus said unto them, 'Because of your unbelief (they could not cast out a demon): for verily I say unto you, If ye have faith as a grain of mustard seed, ye shall say unto this mountain, Remove hence to yonder place; and it shall remove; and nothing shall be impossible unto you.'" Even teeny, tiny mustard-seed-size faith will move mountains. The quality of one's *faith/believe* is not as important as it taking place. Is the switch on?

Then we must ask ourselves, "Why did Jesus marvel at the great faith of the centurion and the Syrophoenician woman?" This author thinks their faith was exceptional because they were gentiles. They had faith even though they did not know Jesus well. We do not know if the centurion ever met Jesus face to face. But he believed in Him! Their faith was out of proportion to their experience of God and His Son. Relative to their knowledge of God they exhibited **great** *faith/believe*! They chose to trust Him who is absolutely trustworthy.

Biblically then, what is important is to decisively and actively *faith/believe* in your heart, now, today.

13 Does Faith Grow?

Many times in the modern church one hears a message or statement about faith growing. Usually, the idea is that the young Christian starts out with **small** faith and then, as he matures, his faith gets **larger**. But is that concept Biblical? And what is the implication of large faith?

First, there is some justification for an individual's faith getting larger in that there is one, and only one, verse in the New Testament which contains the phrase, faith grows. II Thessalonians 1:3 "We are bound to thank God always for you, brethren, as it is meet, because that your **faith grows exceedingly**, and the charity of every one of you all toward each other abounds;"

"Grows exceedingly" is a compound word which is only used once in the Bible, in this verse. However, the root word *auxano* αὐξάνω is used twenty-two times in the New Testament. Studying these other occurrences should give a good understanding of the meaning and usage. The lexicon (Danker) gives the meaning as **become greater, grow, increase.**

Consider the meaning of these verses:

John 3:30, "He must **increase**, but I must decrease." John the Baptist states that Jesus will grow and he, John, will get smaller. We clearly understand that John is talking about Jesus' influence. His following and fame will grow, and John's will diminish. The number of Jesus' followers will increase.

Acts 6:7, "And the word of God **increased**; and the number of the disciples multiplied in Jerusalem greatly; and a great company of the priests were obedient to the faith." We understand in this verse that the author is not saying the Bible got physically bigger, but rather its influence and acceptance increased. The number of those who believed and lived by the Word increased.

Acts 7:17, "But when the time of the promise drew nigh, which God had sworn to Abraham, the people **grew** and multiplied in Egypt," This verse is talking about the number of Israel's descendants increasing. The number of Israelites increased.

Acts 12:24, "But the word of God **grew** and multiplied." The number of those living by the Word increased.

Acts 19:20, "So mightily **grew** the word of God and prevailed." Same.

II Peter 3:18, "But **grow** in grace, and in the knowledge of our Lord and Saviour Jesus Christ. To him be glory both now and for ever. Amen." Does grace itself grow, or rather its influence? Based on usage in other verses, the best interpretation would be that the influence of grace increases numerically. The verb is present, active, imperative, second person, plural. The fact that the verb is plural points to the entire group of brethren to whom he is writing. The number of those living in grace is encouraged, even commanded, to increase.

It is significant that the previous verse uses a plural verb. In the verse in Second Thessalonians the verb is also plural. The verse is addressed to brethren and the pronoun, "your," which proceeds "faith grows" is also plural. Paul is addressing the believers in the church as a group. Based on the usage of *auxano αὐξάνω* in other verses, it appears that the writer is not talking about individual faith itself but rather the influence of faith. The numbers of those believing has increased "exceedingly," (in great measure).

This writer's conclusion is not that an individual believer's faith grows, but rather that the influence of a group of believers increases as they collectively trust God.

14 "I Don't Know (What I Think.)"

✝ ✝ ✝

The author was watching an episode of a 2002 TV series. The wife of one of the regular characters became pregnant. Multiple times the husband was asked what he thought about the pregnancy. His answer was always, "I don't know [what I think about it.]" This answer makes perfect sense in our modern culture. Because every thought and action is emotionalized, an individual must introspectively analyze one's inward state to seriously answer the question. The analysis goes somewhat like this: How do I feel? Am I excited? Am I as excited as I should be? Am I subconsciously resisting the idea? Why? What is my gut telling me?

Obviously this kind of process can go on a long time without any resolution. It went on throughout the entire program. In fact, the character never did come to a resolution. What really shocked me about this was how normal, "I don't know," sounded. How well we relate to this concept. But wait. What do **you** think? **Can** you think? There was no consideration of active decision making here. There was no conviction, no set path of action. The human is powerless in the face of his or her emotions and/or subconscious.

Rather than rational action in thought and deed the person must discover how he feels about the situation. He is helpless. He is in bondage to his emotional reactions. Obviously, this modern man experiences his world passively. He can only react. Action is out of the question. This is the Freudian, emotionalized world that we live in. And it affects each one of us. Moral heroes, men and women of action, are out of fashion. John Wayne, the icon of westerns, is dead. And in a way, so is Jesus. Jesus is now perceived through this introspective lens too. It is all about how **we** experience **Him**, how **we feel** about **Him**.

We don't actively put our trust in God. Rather we introspectively try to analyze whether, and how well, we trust Him. What do we think about God? (Which really means, "How do we feel about God?") How do we feel about the Savior? Do I believe God like Abraham did? To this question one hears the modern church quietly reply, "I don't know." There is no thought of decisive action, only introspective analysis. "I really don't know if I am trusting God like Abraham . . ." Our emotionalized culture has bound our minds with layer upon layer of soft cushy blankets until we can no longer move at all mentally. Finally, the culture has put the church in a straitjacket of psychobabble. Decide? Believe? "I don't know . . .." Jesus said, "Nevertheless when the Son of man comes, will he find faith on the earth?" If faith is passive—emotional—then probably not!

In 1960 Billy Graham launched a magazine for Christians. He and his organization named the new publication Decision Magazine. If the magazine came out today, a good title might be "Influenced," or "(Feel) Close to God." Spiritually speaking we don't seem to make decisions, but rather wait to be influenced by Him. We hope to feel close to God, but we can't make it happen. Some days we feel close and some days we just don't. The whole Christian life is about *feelings*. How can I increase my chances of *feeling close to God*. Yes, read the Bible today. Yes, pray. Yes, go to church.

But these things are not magic. What is the most important action that we should take? John 14:1, "Let not your heart be troubled: ye believe in God, **believe** also in me." Believe in Jesus! Trust God! John 14:11, "**Believe** me that I am in the Father, and the Father in me: or else **believe** me for the very works' sake." Jesus said, "**Believe** me . . ." The verb is present active imperative. **We** are to actively, continually, **believe Him**. It is a command. How can this Biblical idea of transitively, actively, and continually believing God, and His Son be reconciled with the current passive, introspective, wait-for-it, so-called faith of the modern church?

15 Collective Faith

✝ ✝ ✝

In our individualistic culture, it is difficult for one to think collectively, yet in the Bible, collective entities are often the object of God's direct dealings with His created beings. God's first basic unit is the family. Families are important. The spiritual history of a family is important. In Jeremiah 35, God praises the Rechabite family for their adherence to the commands of their ancestor, Jonadab, not to drink wine and to live in tents. God pronounces that there will always be a descendant of the Rechabites that will serve Him.

In the Old Testament, families become countries. There are many examples of God's collective dealing with countries. The foremost example is Israel. From Abraham and Isaac and Israel come the Jewish people. God has worked and will work with them as the sons and daughters of promise. He gave them a land; that's why it is called the

Promised Land. The promise was given to Abraham. What do you do with a promise? The Biblical answer is to believe it, and the One who gave it.

When Israel was delivered out of bondage in Egypt the now millions of descendants of Israel began their journey. They were guided by God to the land He promised them. Twelve prominent men were selected by Moses to spy out this new land. When they returned, they brought good news—and bad news. The land is good, but there will be opposition. At the very moment when Israel should have been receiving that which had been promised, they refused to accept it. Why? As it says in Hebrews 3:19, "So we see that they could not enter in because of unbelief." God's promise was not fulfilled at that time because the people of Israel did not believe in God's character, goodness, and power to accomplish what was promised. Was this failure of faith universal? No, there were several who continued to trust God and encouraged the rest to believe. So, did God let the minority go into the promised land? Yes, but not until forty years later. All Israel had to wander in the desert, even those who trusted God.

What else did God promise Abraham? We talked about the promised land, but God also promised a son. He promised land and descendants to live in that land. Abram, before God changed his name, had a hard time comprehending God's plan, just like we do at times.

When God met with Abram and changed his name to Abraham, He also promised, "As for Sarai thy wife, thou shalt not call her name Sarai, but **Sarah** shall her name be. And I will bless **her**, and give thee a son also **of her**: yea, I will bless **her**, and **she** shall be a mother of nations; kings of people shall be of **her**." When Abraham heard this he was amazed, saying, "Shall a child be born unto him that is an hundred years old? and shall Sarah, that is ninety years old, bear?" Then he says, "O that Ishmael might live before thee!"

This is not the first time God promised Abraham a son. Evidently, for many years, Abraham mistakenly believed that Ishmael was the promised son. Even when given further information, this more complete promise, he wants to hang on to the notion that Ishmael is the son of promise. Abraham is a man of faith, but faith is never perfect. With the heart [**imperfect**] man believes! And God is in the business of clarifying His promises and encouraging our well-founded faith in the One-Who-Is-Absolutely-Trustworthy.

God emphatically repeats, "**Sarah thy wife** shall bear thee a son indeed; and thou shalt call his name Isaac: and I will establish my covenant with him for an everlasting covenant, and with his seed after him." Yes, incredibly, Sarah is going to have a baby, **her** baby, not a surrogate's. And guess what? Abraham believed God. In his heart, he turned on the *faith/believe* switch. To paraphrase, "Yes, God,

I believe."

So, is that it? The following chapter continues the story of faith and the promised son. God and two angels arrive at Abraham's tent. How much time has passed between the chapters? The exact time is unknown, but enough time has passed that Abraham is able to run after being circumcised in the previous chapter. As a good host, Abraham has Sarah prepare a meal for the guests. The menu was fresh baked goods and fresh meat. How long would it take to grind, sift, mix, and bake some bread? How long would it take to locate, select, slaughter, butcher, and cook the meat? Remember there is no refrigeration, no modern stove, and no microwave. The preparation and meal probably took two or three hours. No dialog is recorded until during or after the meal. It is obvious that something very important has brought God himself (a Christophany), and two angels to Abraham's tent. What could it be?

The messengers say to Abraham, "Where is **Sarah thy wife**?" God wants Sarah to become involved. To reinforce, consider the very next verse. **God Himself** says, "I will certainly return unto thee according to the time of life; and, lo, **Sarah thy wife** shall have a son." The promise is emphatically repeated. Why? The very first order of business is Sarah. Notice also that God uses Sarah's new name. And the Bible records that Sarah **hears** what God said, and she laughs when she hears it. (So did Abraham when he heard it in the previous chapter!) And God then says **to Abraham**, "Wherefore did Sarah laugh, saying, Shall I of a surety bear a child, which am old? Is any thing too hard for the LORD? At the time appointed I will return unto thee, according to the time of life, and Sarah shall have a son." This question and promise are directed not at Sarah, but at Abraham. For clarity, let me paraphrase: Abraham! **Why** did Sarah laugh! Is anything **too hard** for me! Surely **Sarah** shall have a **son**!

As I read this portion of scripture and picture the scene, it seems to me that Sarah has not yet heard this vital promise of God. She seems to hear the promise for the first time. She laughs just like Abraham did when he first heard it. This also makes sense when considering God's purpose in the visit. The purpose seems to be that Sarah hear the promise herself. God also seems to be rebuking Abraham for not telling Sarah about the promise. You may, or may not, agree with my interpretation of this passage.

But do not miss the implication for *faith/believe*. Hebrews 11:11 says, "Through faith also **Sara herself** received strength to conceive seed, and was delivered of a child when she was past age, because she judged him faithful who had promised."

It wasn't just Abraham that believed God. ". . . Also Sara herself" believed! Both Dad and Mom believed.

Question: What do you do with a promise?

Answer: **Believe** it because you believe Him!

Sarah heard the promise, and scripture records that she *faith/believe*d the promise. God's promise was fulfilled for Abraham and Sarah because **both** believed.

For the generation of Israel that left Egypt, the promise was delayed to the next generation because the people, as a nation, did not believe. For families, nations, and churches, collective faith in God's promises is vital.

What would have happened if your great-grandfather **and** great-grandmother had believed God and His promises? What would have happened if the pastors **and** congregation of your local church had trusted God specifically according to His promises? As C.S. Lewis said, "No one is ever told that."

But what will happen if a government, a church, a family *believe* God's promises now, today? To paraphrase Lewis, "Anyone can find that out."

Let's find out!!

16 Conclusion

✝ ✝ ✝

What, then, is the conclusion of the matter?

First, that *faith/believe* in God and His promises is the most important action a man or woman can take. The New Testament is full of exhortations to *believe*. Abraham believed God, and so should everyone.

Second, *faith/believe* is an **action** that takes place in the heart. Man believes. It is active, not passive. When the noun, *faith*, is used, its syntax is as a **noun of action**. The noun describes the same action as the verb form. We do not need to wait to trust the Lord. Once we are *faith/believing*, there may be considerable waiting on the Lord, for Him to do the thing that He has lovingly promised, like a land of milk and honey, or a child to enjoy this land. He promised the "coming of our Lord Jesus Christ, and . . . our gathering together unto him." But this is not at all the same as waiting to believe in Him.

Faith: The Believer's Passport

Imagine talking to a baseball player. What would you think if he said, "I'm waiting for a *hit*." You might think that he tends to swing too soon. You ask about his last at-bat. He says that he isn't taking at-bats until he gets a *hit*. "Hey," you say. "*Hit*s don't come in the mail. They don't fall from the sky. You must **swing the bat!**" What a silly example. No baseball player would ever think or act that way. But probably millions of Christians are waiting for God to give them faith, either for themselves or the unsaved around them. But *faith/believe* doesn't come in the mail, and it doesn't fall from the sky. You must *believe* in your heart! Nor do we have to go on a quest to find faith. Romans 10:6b-8, "Who shall ascend into heaven? (that is, to bring Christ down from above:) Or, Who shall descend into the deep? (that is, to bring up Christ again from the dead.) But what saith it? The word is nigh thee, even in thy mouth, and in thy heart: that is, the word of faith, which we preach."

Third, *faith/believe* is transitive. Grammatically, this means the action of *faith/believe* **always** has a subject and an object. Abraham, the subject, believed God, the object. Babe Ruth, the subject, hit the baseball, the object, over the outfield fence. We, the subject, believe God, the object of our faith. *Believe* Him today!

Fourth, *faith/believe* is not an emotion, or a personality trait, or a substance, or a gift, or a corollary, or a work of righteousness. It is never perfect. Only He is perfect. What is important is the object of our *faith/believe*, Him.

Finally, the key to God's power in our lives is *faith/believing* God and the promises found in His Word. Ephesians 1:19 "And what is the exceeding greatness of his power to us-ward who **believe**, according to the working of his mighty power . . ." The verb *believe* in this verse is present tense, denoting continuous and ongoing action. *Faith/believe* is not a onetime event. As we continue to actively trust the Lord, His power becomes active for us and in us. Only when I flip the switch will electricity light the room. Only when I push the accelerator will 3000 pounds of steel begin to move. Don't you want God's power in your life? Don't you need God's power? I do.

Question: Are you *faith/believing* Jesus now, at this moment? A switch is either on or off.

Biblical faith is believing and trusting the character of God and His Word to the extent that one is willing to commit something of value, our life and eternity, into His keeping.

Extra—Questions

†††

1. What is the most important activity or exercise in one's Christian life?
2. What is faith?
3. How does it occur?
4. What are the results of faith?
5. What is the word of faith (in Romans 10)?
6. What are some common misconceptions about faith?
7. When should a Christian believe?
8. How do we partake of God's provision?
9. What do we call the pledges or tokens (vouchers) of that provision?
10. How is a person saved?
11. How does a person know if they are saved?
12. Can a person know if they are saved?

Extra—Hebrews 11: Results of Faith

✝ ✝ ✝

What follows is a list of the results of *faith/believe* from Hebrews 11. Each result is a miracle which happened because ordinary people like you and me put their faith in the God of the Bible. You can add to the list that is in heaven!

1. Hope in God's sure promises (11:1)
2. Certainty about unseen things (11:1)
3. Prepared an ark
4. Condemned the world
5. Became heir
6. Obeyed
7. Sojourned
8. Received strength to conceive
9. Offered a son
10. Blessed a son
11. Blessed sons
12. Worshipped

13. Asked to be buried in Canaan
14. Was hid three months
15. Refused worldly royalty
16. Chose suffering
17. Forsook the world
18. Kept the Passover
19. Passed through the Red Sea
20. Knocked down the walls of Jericho
21. Perished not
22. Won battles
23. Subdued kingdoms
24. Wrought righteousness
25. Obtained promises
26. Stopped the mouth of lions
27. Quenched the fiery furnace
28. Escaped the sword
29. Were made strong when weak
30. Were valiant
31. Made the enemy flee
32. Saw children resurrected
33. Were tortured
34. Were beaten
35. Were put in prison
36. Were stoned
37. Were sawn
38. Endured temptation
39. Wandered destitute
40. Obtained a good report

Extra—Πιστευω Word Study

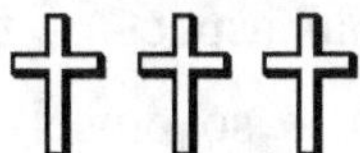

Introduction

This booklet has undertaken the study of the Biblical concept of *faith/believe*. As we have seen, the root word in the original language, Greek, has both nounal and verbal forms, *πιστις* and *πιστευω*. The root word is also used adjectivally and adverbially. Because the verbal idea of action is predominant, this short word study focuses on the verb, *πιστευω*. In the New Testament *πιστευω* is almost always translated *believe*.

Classical usage.

According to Liddell and Scott *πιστευω* means "to trust, trust to or in, put faith in, rely on, believe in a person or thing, or to believe or credit a statement." It is interesting that the classical meaning is so close to the New Testament. The verb is transitive with the usual object either a person, or a statement by a person. The personal aspect then is fairly narrow and defined. For contrast, one might possibly πιστευω or believe in a machine like a car, or an animal like a horse; but the usage is typically personal and relates to another human being.

In ancient grammatical usage the object of <u>πιστευω</u> was usually a noun in the dative case. The dative case in general references personal relationship, so the dative further emphasizes the relational aspect of the verb. "Some verbs have a root idea which is so closely related to that of the dative that they take their direct object in the dative rather than the accusative case."[4] Later, the preposition εν sometimes appeared before the dative object. Later still, the preposition changed to εις, and the case of the object changed to the accusative. Thus, to believe someone changed to believe in someone.

In the New Testament, there are examples of the both the simple dative object, and the accusative object preceded by εις.

Ancient papyri usage

In the active voice there are examples in the papyri of one person trusting another, or more often **not** trusting someone. In the passive voice one is entrusted with a situation or duty. A cited example is Paul being entrusted

---

[4] Brooks and Winbery, *Syntax of New Testament Greek* (Lanham, MD: University Press, 1979), 37.

with the Gospel.[5] Evidently trust is typically viewed as one way, one person to another. Because of this, the use of plenary genitive with πιστις is unlikely since it would imply two-way trust.

An interesting aspect is that one trusts another with the expectation of a future result. Would you loan your car to someone that you distrust? No, but because you trust your cousin, you lend him your car expecting that that he will take good care of it and return it in good condition. It follows then that πιστευω implies a considered personal investment on the part of the one granting trust. It is not flippantly given. Something of value is on the line.

But in our relationship with God, how can the believer invest anything? He has nothing of value to give to the One-Who-Needs-Nothing. But God knows of something that every person **should** value above everything else in their sphere of experience—their soul, their life, their future, their eternal destination. Because of the great love of One, for those who did not know their danger, Jesus came and died.

Septuagint usage

The Hebrew word <u>H539</u> (and 540) אָמַן' âman in most cases is the predecessor for πιστευω in the Septuagint.

Πιστευω is used forty-eight times in forty-seven verses in the Septuagint. A partial list of references is as follows:

---

[5] Moulton Milligan, *Vocabulary of The Greek Testament* (London: Hodder and Stoughton, 1929), 514

(Genesis 15:6) And he believedH539 in the LORD;H3068 and he countedH2803 it to him for righteousness.H6666

(Genesis 42:20) But bringH935 your youngestH6996 brotherH251 untoH413 me; so shall your wordsH1697 be verified,H539 and ye shall notH3808 die.H4191 And they didH6213 so.H3651

(Genesis 45:26) And toldH5046 him, saying,H559 JosephH3130 is yetH5750 alive,H2416 and heH1931 is governorH4910 over allH3605 the landH776 of Egypt.H4714 And Jacob's heartH3820 fainted,H6313 forH3588 he believedH539 them not.H3808

(Exodus 4:1) And MosesH4872 answeredH6030 and said,H559 But, behold,H2005 they will notH3808 believeH539 me, norH3808 hearkenH8085 unto my voice:H6963 forH3588 they will say,H559 The LORDH3068 hath notH3808 appearedH7200 untoH413 thee.

(Exodus 4:5) ThatH4616 they may believeH539 thatH3588 the LORDH3068 GodH430 of their fathers,H1 the GodH430 of Abraham,H85 the GodH430 of Isaac,H3327 and the GodH430 of Jacob,H3290 hath appearedH7200 untoH413 thee.

(Exodus 4:8) And it shall come to pass,H1961 ifH518 they will notH3808 believeH539 thee, neitherH3808 hearkenH8085 to the voiceH6963 of the firstH7223 sign,H226 that they will believeH539 the voiceH6963 of the latterH314 sign.H226

(Exodus 4:9) And it shall come to pass,H1961 ifH518 they will notH3808 believeH539 alsoH1571 theseH428 twoH8147 signs,H226 neitherH3808 hearkenH8085 unto thy voice,H6963 that thou shalt takeH3947 of the waterH4480 H4325 of the river,H2975 and pourH8210 it upon the dryH3004 land: and the waterH4325 whichH834 thou takestH3947 out ofH4480 the riverH2975 shall becomeH1961 bloodH1818 upon the dryH3006 land.

(Exodus 4:31) And the peopleH5971 believed:H539 and when they heardH8085 thatH3588 the LORDH3068 had visitedH6485 (H853) the childrenH1121 of Israel,H3478 and thatH3588 he had looked uponH7200 (H853) their affliction,H6040 then they bowed their headsH6915 and worshipped.H7812

(Exodus 14:31) And IsraelH3478 sawH7200 (H853) that greatH1419 workH3027 whichH834 the LORDH3068 didH6213 upon the Egyptians:H4714 and the peopleH5971 fearedH3372 (H853) the LORD,H3068 and believedH539 the LORD,H3068 and his servantH5650 Moses.H4872

(Exodus 19:9) And the LORDH3068 saidH559 untoH413 Moses,H4872 Lo,H2009 IH595 comeH935 untoH413 thee in a thickH5645 cloud,H6051 thatH5668 the peopleH5971 may hearH8085 when I speakH1696 withH5973 thee, and believeH539 thee for ever.H5769 And MosesH4872 toldH5046 (H853) the wordsH1697 of the peopleH5971 untoH413 the LORD.H3068

(Numbers 14:11) And the LORDH3068 saidH559 untoH413 Moses,H4872 How longH5704 H575 will thisH2088 peopleH5971 provokeH5006 me? and how longH5704 H575 will it be ereH3808 they believeH539 me, for allH3605 the signsH226 whichH834 I have shewedH6213 amongH7130 them?

(Numbers 20:12) And the LORDH3068 spakeH559 untoH413 MosesH4872 and Aaron,H175 BecauseH3282 ye believedH539 me not,H3808 to sanctifyH6942 me in the eyesH5869 of the childrenH1121 of Israel,H3478 thereforeH3651 ye shall notH3808 bringH935 (H853) thisH2088 congregationH6951 intoH413 the landH776 whichH834 I have givenH5414 them.

(Deuteronomy 9:23) Likewise when the LORDH3068 sentH7971 you from Kadeshbarnea,H4480 H6947 saying,H559 Go upH5927 and possessH3423 (H853) the landH776 whichH834 I have givenH5414 you; then ye rebelled againstH4784 (H853) the commandmentH6310 of the LORDH3068 your God,H430 and ye believedH539 him not,H3808 norH3808 hearkenedH8085 to his voice.H6963

(Deuteronomy 28:66) And thy lifeH2416 shall hangH1961 in doubtH8511 beforeH4480 H5048 thee; and thou shalt fearH6342 dayH3119 and night,H3915 and shalt have none assuranceH539 H3808 of thy life:H2416

(1 Samuel 3:21) And the LORDH3068 appearedH7200 againH3254 in Shiloh:H7887 forH3588 the LORDH3068 revealed himselfH1540 toH413 SamuelH8050 in ShilohH7887 by the wordH1697 of the LORD.H3068

(1 Samuel 27:12) And AchishH397 believedH539 David,H1732 saying,H559 He hath made his peopleH5971 IsraelH3478 utterly to abhorH887 H887 him; therefore he shall beH1961 my servantH5650 for ever.H5769

(1 Kings 10:7) Howbeit I believedH539 notH3808 the words,H1697 untilH5704 H834 I came,H935 and mine eyesH5869 had seenH7200 it: and, behold,H2009 the halfH2677 was notH3808 toldH5046 me: thy wisdomH2451 and prosperityH2896 exceedethH3254 H413 the fameH8052

whichH834 I heard.H8085

(2 Chronicles 9:6) Howbeit I believedH539 notH3808 their words,H1697 untilH5704 H834 I came,H935 and mine eyesH5869 had seenH7200 it: and, behold,H2009 the one halfH2677 of the greatnessH4768 of thy wisdomH2451 was notH3808 toldH5046 me: for thou exceedestH3254 H5921 the fameH8052 thatH834 I heard.H8085

(2 Chronicles 32:15) NowH6258 therefore let notH408 HezekiahH2396 deceiveH5377 you, norH408 persuadeH5496 you on this manner,H2063 neitherH408 yet believeH539 him: forH3588 noH3808 H3605 godH433 of anyH3605 nationH1471 or kingdomH4467 was ableH3201 to deliverH5337 his peopleH5971 out of mine hand,H4480 H3027 and out of the handH4480 H3027 of my fathers:H1 how much lessH637 H3588 shall your GodH430 deliverH5337 you out of mine hand?H4480 H3027

(Job 4:18) Behold,H2005 he put no trustH539 H3808 in his servants;H5650 and his angelsH4397 he chargedH7760 with folly:H8417

(Job 9:16) IfH518 I had called,H7121 and he had answeredH6030 me; yet would I notH3808 believeH539 thatH3588 he had hearkenedH238 unto my voice.H6963

(Job 15:15) Behold,H2005 he putteth no trust<u>H539</u> H3808 in his saints;H6918 yea, the heavensH8064 are notH3808 cleanH2141 in his sight.H5869

(Job 15:22) He believeth<u>H539</u> notH3808 that he shall returnH7725 out ofH4480 darkness,H2822 and heH1931 is waited forH6822 ofH413 the sword.H2719

(Job 15:31) Let notH408 him that is deceivedH8582 trust<u>H539</u> in vanity:H7723 forH3588 vanityH7723 shall beH1961 his recompence.H8545

(Job 24:22) He drawethH4900 also the mightyH47 with his power:H3581 he riseth up,H6965 and noH3808 man is sure<u>H539</u> of life.H2416

(Job 29:24) If I laughedH7832 onH413 them, they believed<u>H539</u> it not;H3808 and the lightH216 of my countenanceH6440 they cast not down.H5307 H3808

(Job 39:12) Wilt thou believe<u>H539</u> him, thatH3588 he will bring homeH7725 thy seed,H2233 and gatherH622 it into thy barn?H1637

(Job 39:24) He swalloweth H1572 the groundH776 with fiercenessH7494 and rage:H7267 neitherH3808 believeth<u>H539</u> he thatH3588 it is the soundH6963 of the trumpet.H7782

(Psalms 27:13/26:13Septuagint) I had fainted, unlessH3884 I had believedH539 to seeH7200 the goodnessH2898 of the LORDH3068 in the landH776 of the living.H2416

(Psalms 78:22/77:22Septuagint) BecauseH3588 they believedH539 notH3808 in God,H430 and trustedH982 notH3808 in his salvation:H3444

(Psalms 78:32/77:32Septuagint) For allH3605 thisH2063 they sinnedH2398 still,H5750 and believedH539 notH3808 for his wondrous works.H6381

(Psalms 106:12/105:12Septuagint) Then believedH539 they his words;H1697 they sangH7891 his praise.H8416

(Psalms 106:24/105:24Septuagint) Yea, they despisedH3988 the pleasantH2532 land,H776 they believedH539 notH3808 his word:H1697

(Psalms 116:10/115:1Septuagint) I believed,H539 thereforeH3588 have IH589 spoken:H1696 I was greatlyH3966 afflicted:H6031

(Psalms 119:66) TeachH3925 me goodH2898 judgmentH2940 and

knowledge:H1847 forH3588 I have believedH539 thy commandments.H4687

(Proverbs 14:15) The simpleH6612 believethH539 everyH3605 word:H1697 but the prudentH6175 man looketh wellH995 to his going.H838

(Isaiah 7:9) And the headH7218 of EphraimH669 is Samaria,H8111 and the headH7218 of SamariaH8111 is Remaliah'sH7425 son.H1121 IfH518 ye will notH3808 believe,H539 surelyH3588 ye shall notH3808 be established.H539

(Isaiah 28:16) ThereforeH3651 thusH3541 saithH559 the LordH136 GOD,H3069 Behold,H2009 I layH3245 in ZionH6726 for a foundationH3245 a stone,H68 a triedH976 stone,H68 a preciousH3368 cornerH6438 stone, a sureH3245 foundation:H4143 he that believethH539 shall notH3808 make haste.H2363

(Isaiah 43:10) YeH859 are my witnesses,H5707 saithH5002 the LORD,H3068 and my servantH5650 whomH834 I have chosen:H977 thatH4616 ye may knowH3045 and believeH539 me, and understandH995 thatH3588 IH589 am he:H1931 beforeH6440 me there was noH3808 GodH410 formed,H3335 neitherH3808 shall there beH1961 afterH310 me.

(Isaiah 53:1) WhoH4310 hath believedH539 our report?H8052 and toH5921 whomH4310 is the armH2220 of the LORDH3068 revealed?H1540

(Jeremiah 12:6) ForH3588 evenH1571 thy brethren,H251 and the houseH1004 of thy father,H1 evenH1571 theyH1992 have dealt treacherouslyH898 with thee; yea,H1571 theyH1992 have calledH7121 a multitudeH4392 afterH310 thee: believeH539 them not,H408 thoughH3588 they speakH1696 fair wordsH2896 untoH413 thee.

(Jeremiah 25:8) ThereforeH3651 thusH3541 saithH559 the LORDH3068 of hosts;H6635 BecauseH3282 H834 ye have notH3808 heardH8085 (H853) my words,H1697

(Lamentations 4:12) The kingsH4428 of the earth,H776 and allH3605 the inhabitantsH3427 of the world,H8398 would notH3808 have believedH539 thatH3588 the adversaryH6862 and the enemyH341 should have enteredH935 into the gatesH8179 of Jerusalem.H3389

(Daniel 6:23) ThenH116 was the king exceeding gladH4430 H7690 H2868 forH5922 him, and commandedH560 that they should take Daniel upH5267 H1841 out

> ofH4481 the den.H1358 So DanielH1841 was taken upH5267 out ofH4481 the den,H1358 and no mannerH3809 H3606 of hurtH2257 was foundH7912 upon him, becauseH1768 he believedH540 in his God.H426

> (Habakkuk 1:5) BeholdH7200 ye among the heathen,H1471 and regard,H5027 and wonder marvellously:H8539 H8539 forH3588 I will workH6466 a workH6467 in your days,H3117 which ye will notH3808 believe,<u>H539</u> thoughH3588 it be toldH5608 you.

In almost every case the Hebrew word translated $\pi\iota\sigma\tau\epsilon\upsilon\omega$ is אָמַן' âman. It means to *render* (or *be*) *firm* or faithful, to *trust* or believe, to be *permanent* or quiet; morally to *be true* or certain; once (in Isaiah 30:21; by interchange for H541) to *go to the right hand:* - hence assurance, believe, bring up, establish, + fail, be faithful (of long continuance, stedfast, sure, surely, trusty, verified), nurse, (-ing father), (put), trust, turn to the right. (Esword H539)

New Testament Usage

This booklet is itself a study of the New Testament usage of the root word, ΠΙΣΤ. To $\pi\iota\sigma\tau\epsilon\upsilon\omega$ is to believe and trust the character of another to the extent that one is willing to commit something of value into his keeping. With the heart man believes God and His promises.

Summary

Faith: The Believer's Passport

Πιστευω is a transitive verb. It usually describes a personal transaction whereby the subject believes or trusts the character or statement of another person. A future result is expected. Something of value is at stake. The Biblical paradigm is the very first verse where *πιστευω* appears in the Septuagint.

> (Genesis 15:6) And he (Abraham) believed in the LORD; and he (the Lord) counted it to him for righteousness.

Abraham believed God with his future and the futures of his descendants, even including Jesus himself. He believed that God would provide a land for these descendants. This was not pie-in-the-sky. Based on God's promises he moved his family. He circumcised all the males under his direction. He even was willing to sacrifice his own son, all because he trusted and believed God. He entrusted Him with everything of value, everything! Will you? Will we?

> (2 Timothy 1:12) For the which cause I also suffer these things: nevertheless I am not ashamed: for **I know whom I have believed**, and am persuaded that **he is able to keep that which I have committed unto him against that day.**

When we believe Him we commit something of value into His hand. The amazing thing is that only He truly knows the value and importance of what we are putting in His hand. He is the only one who can care for and protect us—our life, our soul, our eternal destination. Only He sees true reality. Only He is able. Only He is trustworthy. Only He is the proper object of our *Πιστις*, our faith. *Πιστευω* Him!

Extra—Tests of Faith:

1. Is it an action?
2. Does it take place in one's heart?
3. When did the action take place?
4. Is it transitive?
5. Is the subject a person, usually man or woman?
6. Is the object God, or His promise or statement?
7. Is the action active or middle voice?
8. Is there a result? Caution: the result may take a while and may not be immediate. In fact, the result may be decades later. Don't confuse results with *faith* itself.

Faith: The Believer's Passport

Extra—Facts about Faith

It might be helpful to list some facts about faith as it is presented in the Bible. These are not opinions, but rather little-known facts. Most of these items come from a knowledge of Greek, the language God chose for the New Testament.

1. The Greek word for *faith* used in the New Testament is *pistis*, a noun.
2. *Pistis* is similar in usage to the Greek word, *agape*, meaning *love*.
3. Both these nouns are technically called "nouns of action." They are nouns which describe or picture an action. Both nouns are typically followed by a noun in the genitive case. That following word is either the subject (subjective genitive), or the object (objective genitive) of the action pictured by the "noun of action." This grammatical construction has a few carryovers in English. E.g., "*love* of money" or "forgiveness of sins." These English phrases could be paraphrased as "one loves money;" or "one forgives sins."
4. In the New Testament *agape* and *pistis* have these verb forms, *agapao* and *pisteuo*,

respectively. In English, we understand that *love* or *agape/agapao* is both a noun and a verb. But this is not the case with *pistis/pisteuo* because *pisteuo* is typically translated *believe*. *Faith,* in the Bible, then is a "noun of action" which pictures an action.

5. The root word for *faith/believe* occurs over six hundred times in the New Testament. For comparison, the root word for love occurs a little over three hundred times. *Pistis/pisteuo*, or *faith/believe* is an extremely important word.

6. Romans 10:10 For with the heart man **believeth** unto righteousness; and with the mouth confession is made unto salvation.

7. Man believes.

8. Romans 4:3 For what saith the scripture? Abraham **believed** God, and it was counted unto him for righteousness.

9. Abraham, a man, believed God.

10. *Faith*/believe is an action which takes place in the heart of a man.

11. *Faith*/believe is typically in the active or middle voice, rarely the passive voice. In other words, faith/believe is not something that happens to you, but rather something that I/you/we do. Grammatically, we initiate the action. (Of course, God is drawing us toward that action, but I am trying diligently to stick to the facts.) Abraham believed God. Babe Ruth hit the baseball. Tom Brady threw a touchdown.

12. In Greek, like Spanish, nouns have particular genders. The phrase, *la casa, the house*, is an article, *the*, followed by the noun, *house*. The Spanish word for *the* is either *el*, which is masculine, or *la*, which is feminine. *Casa, house*, is feminine and therefore preceded by *la*. The phrase *el casa* is incorrect. The article, or pronoun, or adjective must match the gender of the noun it modifies.

13. Ephesians 2:8 "For by **grace** are you saved through **faith**: and **that** not of yourselves: **it** is the **gift** of God." In Greek, there are three genders, masculine, feminine, and neuter. Nouns and their modifiers must match in gender. *Grace* and *faith* are both feminine gender. *That* is neuter. *It* is understood and refers to *that*. *That* cannot refer to either *grace* or *faith* because the genders do not match. *That* is referring to the action of the verb, saved. The gift is the entire process of salvation. It—being saved—is God's GREAT GIFT.

Just the facts.

www.ingramcontent.com/pod-product-compliance
Lightning Source LLC
Chambersburg PA
CBHW072103150726
47999CB00005B/1861